traces of love

MADELINE ROSALES

authorHOUSE®

AuthorHouse™
1663 Liberty Drive
Bloomington, IN 47403
www.authorhouse.com
Phone: 1 (800) 839-8640

Published by AuthorHouse 07/09/2018

ISBN: 978-1-5462-5009-8 (sc)
ISBN: 978-1-5462-5007-4 (hc)
ISBN: 978-1-5462-5008-1 (e)

Library of Congress Control Number: 2018907977

Print information available on the last page.

Any people depicted in stock imagery provided by Getty Images are models,
and such images are being used for illustrative purposes only.
Certain stock imagery © Getty Images.

This book is printed on acid-free paper.

Because of the dynamic nature of the Internet, any web addresses or links contained in
this book may have changed since publication and may no longer be valid. The views
expressed in this work are solely those of the author and do not necessarily reflect the
views of the publisher, and the publisher hereby disclaims any responsibility for them.

contents

dedication

I dedicate this book to all "furry, feathered and woolly
beauties of the animal kingdom" with their love they
come to rejoice the life leaving large footprints in it
and which are usually expressed beyond words.
Also, to all those who have sacrificed their
lives to save or defend their masters.

acknowledgments

Thanks to Norah, Demian and Ismael, my beloved family for being always by my side, brighten my life, giving me their love, support, and the time required to complete this book and to be my source of inspiration.

introduction

Through the evolution of the world there have been changes of all kinds, our way of thinking and our relationships have also changed, not only among human beings but also between humans and animals. Just a few decades ago, many pets were suffering terribly from negligence, abuse and exploitation, among other things. There were places in which the families didn't have a clear sense of responsibility, these people only thought how to get economic benefits with animals. Some owners do not use preventive cares such as sterilization, vaccination and deworming; because, in those times, veterinary care costs were very expensive and there were just a few of them, especially in communities with medium or low incomes, so it was hard for them to spend money in pet's health because it was not a priority choice, "those are things for rich people" they said.

They also believed that animals did not have emotions, feelings, intelligence, or even soul. This way of thinking procured to these lovely creatures much suffering in their lives. On the other hand, the great use and abuse in their bodies forcing them to procreate as many times as possible to make great business with puppies, the lack of attention and no periodic medical reviews culminated in the development of diseases that ended with their lives, most of the times at an early age.

As the years have passed, fortunately we have seen noticeable changes in the way we see and treat a pet. This is very good because it means that we have been sensitized and we have taken the time to look at them "closer" and realize that they are neither insensitive nor irrational not without mentioning that they have great intelligence and personality.

It is well known today by professional coaches that the development of intelligence in any animal is a result of a loving foster care by the owner; that is, when you are treated with dignity, respect and love. This also strengthens the ties between the human and the pet, and creates confidence, security and the development of a unique and own personality.

However, there are cultures that simply do not conceive that the behavior of an animal could be out of the standards considered as "normal". This can lead to some degree of fear, which creates reactions of aggression and violence.

This book intends to show four lives from different pets that lived at different times: Sparky lived at the beginning of the 80's, Claudio was born in the middle 80's, while Giacomo lived at the end of the first decade of 2000's and Thumbelina was born in the middle of the second decade of the 2000's.

In each of the stories we will see very different ways of treating a pet and you will be able to appreciate different behaviors, emotions and characters in each one of our protagonists. The only constant in all of them: the gratitude and loyalty to the human being.

Regardless of the gender, breed, size or shape of an animal, we could look into their eyes and discover the purity of their souls and feel their unconditional love, we could write an entire book for every one of them, full of teachings for us humans. Animals can give us lessons on how to go about live without complications, and drama. No matter how hard live experience may be, they will always face challenges with great attitude towards live.

I am sure that, if you've ever had a pet, you also have a great story to tell the world.

sparky

My story begins when I came to this world; I don't remember my mom, I was too young even when I was turned away from her. It was the custom of the place where I was born to move the cubs from her mother as soon as possible after birth, or at least until they could eat themselves. This is sad because you feel unprotected and lonely, your siblings to play and have fun are not with you either.

Fortunately for me, I was given to a home where they were cordial and even a little loving with me, it was a family with 7 young siblings among teenagers and adults. At first, the girls took care of me and treated me with affection, but as I grew up I felt that was already well adapted to my new home and stopped giving me so much attention and care.

Before my new independence, I decided to explore the grounds of my new house, of which I knew only a very small part. Little by little I ventured to go beyond.

I discovered that beyond the house, (which would be called back yard) was a huge place in which the father of my new owners planted some crops, there were also many flowers and other plants with strange smells but used for the family to make tea. I had fun long hours exploring and observing how other small animals called Grasshoppers jumped between the fields and the grass. I also found other small houses within the same field, but it was still too shy to go to them.

A few months since I had arrived, I became a Maltese very nice and polite (or at least I heard that it was said about me for my owners when other people knew me), I liked to eat cleanly, and be discreet when making my needs, never played with the things of my owners (although sometimes it was tempting to nibble one than other shoe or play with the hanging clothes on the clothesline), because I knew those things were precious for them.

Little by little, I began to look more closely at the neighboring houses. In one of those, was living a cat little warm and no gentle that did not allow me the access. This feline was the cause I hate its kind.

It was a day in which I was making my usual rounds, I relied on the kindness of the cat. Very politely I greeted him I said:

- Hello, I am Sparky and I live next to your door, I'm your neighbor it is a pleasure to meet you, what is your name?

For my painful surprise, this ill-mannered pussycat received me with a claw directly to my eye. Fortunately, my reaction was more or less quickly and I could move so fast that I wasn't half blind, the damage was reduced to a tremendous scratch on the inside of the eyelid, which was invested permanently, I never received any attention to heal, which caused me discomfort, a little blooding and pain for the rest of my life, as it always carved to find some relief. From that moment ended my good relationship with cats and I kept in a constant fight with them.

After this painful episode, drew my attention to another of the houses and began my cautious approach. The perceived as the leader of the flock; I mean, the mother, timid, and noticed my frequent visits. She invited me occasionally to eat, because apparently, I liked:

- Hey little, poor you! What happened to your eye? are you hungry? Would you like to taste some food?

Of course, I accepted willingly and with deep pain I tried to explain my embarrassing encounter with that killer crazy cat.

I liked to go that house, because there were a couple of little kids with whom was nice to interact, the bigger was 5 years and the small one was 3 years old. I became to be a frequent visit to that house, until one day I didn't go back to my old home. My previous owners seemed not to worry or bother them much my absence, and by my way, I enjoyed the days having fun with the cubs, sun myself pleasantly on the lawn and out occasionally to socialize with other neighborhood friends. Everything was perfect, with the exception of when my new owner who considered that it was a little out of alignment and decided to give me a bath.

It was the most terrible thing!!! I was trimmed and

bathed with hair shampoo with a horrible smell and COLD
WATER!!!

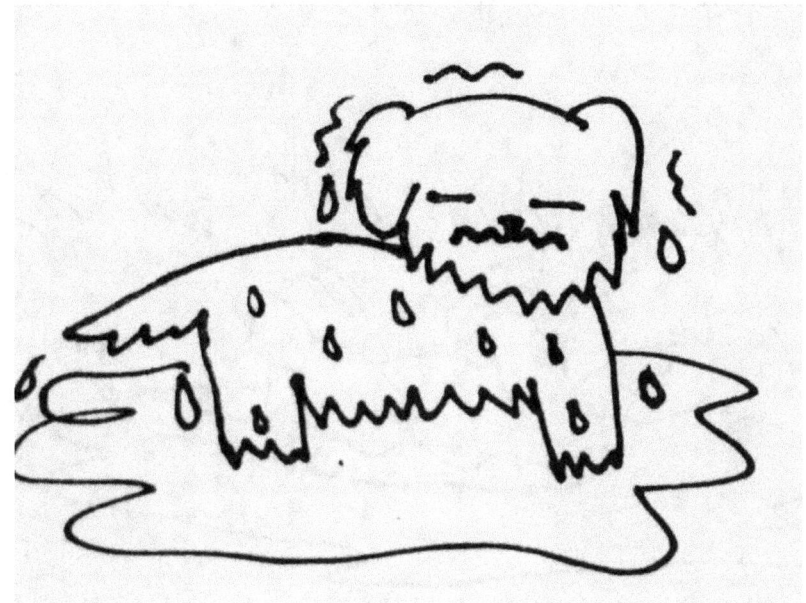

Then, the fun and pleasant part came when I escaped
running towards the field and I rolled in the mud to dry
myself. As soon as saw me coming back, they tried to catch
me while I was screaming:

- Spark! - Come here! - you are in so much trouble dear!
  You have to take a bath!
- Whaaaat? Another bath? Oooohhh Noooo! Never
  mind!

Of course, they couldn't catch me, because I was much faster than them. Once I dried, I shook my body and all the dust came out easily all over me, as clean as after the bath.

My life was good for a few months until my canine friends came and met me. I found one cute dog that was going to become the father of my first puppies. After a few weeks, it was a strange feeling, suddenly wasn't as agile as I used to be and I slept more time too.

On the other hand, I had a lot of appetite and I felt something moving inside my belly and it was growing up. As the days go by, I felt increasingly fatigued, so I looked for a cozy corner to hide and be alone.

Finally, after much pain my puppies were born, they were five small ones.

My family was aware of the event and the kids were very happy, but their parents weren't so much. After all, they were patient and tolerant because they were paying attention and caring a new child that had just been born too. For this reason, they began to look for people who wanted to adopt my puppies, and one by one they were given away except for the last one that unfortunately did not survive.

Once again, my life was as before. After this event a few months went by and again I wanted to get out of the house. My owners noticed that and they did not allow me to leave. I had to find a way to duck by the hallway while they drew their car or when they opened the door in case someone rang the bell. Finally, when I ran to the street they were yelling at me to come back, but I didn't. So, there were more puppies and that began to be a problem for the family, because people can accept a puppy once, but no more. In addition to that, the mother was too busy with the new baby, that the middle daughter felt a little abandoned by her. I clearly remember one occasion in which the little girl was sad because her mother didn't attend and care for her as she needed, so she decided to take refuge with me. On that time, she just took all of my puppies far away from me, and that was so sad for me, I had no longer who to care for or feed. She approached quietly to me and began to tell me very sad that his mom didn't love her any more, now the mother just wanted the new baby and that she had ceased to be the baby in the house, I listen attentively and gave him a slobbery kiss as consolation, she thanked me instantly telling me:

– Thanks Sparky, do you love me?

To which I replied with another lick. She immediately said:

– Sparky, do you want to be my mom?

My answer was the same as the previous ones, she thanked me once more and asked me to feed her. She made herself comfortable as my puppies used to do it and she began to drink from my milk. I just took her in as I did with my puppies. Once she felt better she thanked me again wishing I would have been her mom and she arranged to get in the house.

Shortly, after I began to be a burden for the parents of the family. They didn't speak so lovingly to me anymore, if I went out to the street they wouldn't allow me to enter the house, or they welcome my return with a beating.

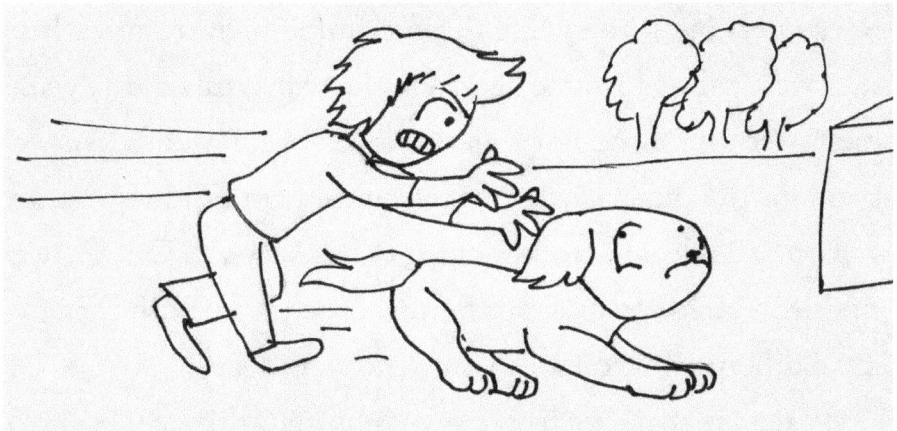

This situation became increasingly frequent, sometimes found refuge with some sisters who visited frequently to the children of my owners, their cousins. I was tried for them with true affection and respect, I remember that I was invited to go to her house which was a few blocks from mine. They asked permission to the mother to take me, and she accessed without problem. In a very short time I learned the way to their house, which was my refuge when things got bad on mine. When I wanted to shovel, fleeing and ran non-stop until the other house. When the girls saw me out when they opened the door asked:

- What happened to you Sparky? Why did you come? Do they hurt you?

I could tell my face told everything. My life had been always like this, give birth to a new offspring in which at least one of them passed away, and a thrashing given to me from my owners once in a while. I sometimes ran away and when they were calmed I came back. Finally, the family didn't want me to return. Although I always loved them and I thanked them for the time they let me live with them I didn't want to go back; so I decided to stay at the cousins' house. Only, when the girls visited my previous family, I used to go with them to my old home. But only to visit them not to stay.

I can't say that the change was completely different because the grandmother didn't like the animals at all, when she saw I didn't come back to my old house, she told the girls in an angry way:

- Isn't that flea-ridden dog going back to her house? - I don't want it here!

But the girls, they wanted me to stay there, so in spite of the grandmother I stayed. They treated me with a lot of love, give me some candy, food, they washed and cut my hair; although that part did not change much, because at the end

I was escaping to go to the delicious earth to roll up for take away the cold. They were building houses cozy and warm on chilly days, because the dogs we were not allowed to enter and sleep inside the house.

The years that I was allowed to lived in that house due the love these young people expressed were great. As it is common in our species, I corresponded with loyalty and gratitude to his affection because it is well known that the canines are a kind that often give their lives for their masters. I think they were interested in me, so much that at times we could engage in long conversations in which they expressed their feelings towards me. Despite not sharing the same language, we understood each other well.

However, abuse and negligence from the grandmother and

sometimes by the mother continued in my life, fortunately they were not as hard as the previous owners but it was inevitable I escape to the street once in a while. In some cases, the punishment was to keep me out, so I had to sleep in the street, or they could get me wet with ice water or receive me with the blow of a broom. Finally, they tried to drive off my visits spraying me with a perfume scent so strong and unpleasant that I don't know how I didn't spoil my smell, because the odor was so intense that could be perceived several streets away. In my desperation to get rid of that smell I spent hours scrubbing mainly my rear on the ground, floor mats, or where I could. But it was useless, that smell would not go off from my coat in many days. The only good thing from this situation is that flies were far away from me.

The stories of my puppies were going from bad to worse because they were not wanted by the grandmother and the mother. They were advised by some neighbors who devised ways to get rid of them such as abandon them in a vacant lot far away from the house or send someone to do it for them. Despite my sadness, I went ahead although I also wondered why people can hurt such innocent creatures? Why do they want to end up with their lives as if they were worth nothing? I never understood why sometimes people is so cruel with us.

The day finally came when they considered that the solution was to get rid of me and they entrusted a person to put me in a sack and took me away to leave me there. And it was done. An unknown man got me into a sack and in a car, he took me to a place far away from the house and get me out of the sack, he went up to the car and left me there abandoned. I didn't know where I was, but my sense of smell could help me find the way to home. It is well known that the dogs we are guided by the smell more than any other sense. It took me a couple of days to go back because to find the way back was not an easy task. I finally got to the house almost dead of hunger, thirst and fatigue, when they saw me I perceive two reactions: the first one was the mother and grandmother who were astonished and said:

- Danged it! What on earth is this? How did you get back spark?

On the other hand, the face of the girls with happiness for my return, they also exclaimed:

- Sparky! What a joy, thank you for coming back! You're very Smart Little one!

The girls helped me to enter and they quickly gave me something to eat and water, while they were asking me if I was fine. The next day they gave me a bath followed by a meal so that I could get strong again. That episode was my salvation, because they gave up and stopped trying to find a way to get rid of me.

My stay in that house was due to the fact that we the dogs, are faithful and also grateful until death, the girls loved me and in spite of many things, it was worth to stay in the house for them; they would have liked to have done more for me, but their petitions in defense of mine were simply ignored. Whatever, I have to recognize that the abuse was reduced a little bit when I demonstrated my intelligence and loyalty to family returning home alone without help.

- If only they could hear me! I thought. I wanted to say in many ways that I did not intend to get dirty when I walked into the house, that it was not my intention to bother them when I went out to the street, that it is my nature and an instinct to survive of my species and to give life to new beings. In spite of the fact that sometimes they hurt me with their indifference and coldness their punishments or when they had a grudge against me, I was very grateful that they gave me a small corner in their home and the love and attention that I received from my young owners.

Sometimes I thought that one of them could bring some communication among us, I had the feeling that she understood when I wanted to say something, it was enough to look at me directly to the eyes and she knew what I wanted to tell her. I think that it is the most effective way to initiate a connection with us, the animals, and also with humans too.

How many times have you seen the expression of the eyes

in others guessing how they feel? There is a saying: "the eyes are the window to the soul", I really think, that's right!

There were days much better than others. For example, when I was invited to pass into the living room for a few moments after having received a bath, or when the girls shared their food with me. Also, I loved some celebrations such as birthdays because they gave me a bit of cake; or in Christmas when there was a lot of food left over and It was a feast for me. I loved too the "piñatas", because when they were broken, I tried to get as many sweetmeats as I could, and also some fruit and nuts. Of course, I always managed to catch enough for some days.

I also remember that on Christmas they always made a welcoming manger in which they bed down a child that they called Jesus after celebrating his birth. They had figurines of people around, also many kinds of animals, and was full of lights around it and a large and warm focus within the little house, and in the center a cozy bed with soft cotton which invited me to stay on it. Carefully, I went into the crib and without intention to disturb I would curl up next to the child that was lying down there. What could be wrong with a bit of heat in exchange for having the most comfortable?

Of course, many times I jumped out when I heard a cry that said:

- SPARK!!! WHAT THE HELL ARE YOU DOING NEXT TO THE CHILD JESUS???

Of course, when I heard the screams I ran away in great anguish.

I also remember a fig tree in the back yard, from which I enjoyed it's figs when the ripeness make them to fall by themselves from the branches and its refreshing shade under which I spent hours sleeping. That was so good. What days, the most peaceful and happy of my existence.

I remember an episode that, at the beginning, it was not only mysterious but happiest also funny. It was after midnight on a common day, everything was absolute peaceful and quiet, I was sleeping in the courtyard as always when I suddenly heard up a terrible noise coming from the kitchen, it was as if all the pots had fallen down at the same time from the cupboard. Right away, I ran barking as tightly as I could to scare the intruder and warning that best outside, but when I used my smell I simply did not perceive the presence of any strange; anyway, I kept barking and I didn't know what or whom had been. After a few minutes running to see what had happened, they carefully entered to the kitchen, I was in front of them barking bravely and when they turn on the light, Oh, what a surprise! There was no one or nothing lying on the ground, everything was in perfect order and in its place. As you can imagine, my owners were nearly gooseflesh and ran out screaming that there were ghosts in the house. That scene was very funny and made me have a certain respect for being very brave in the face of the ghosts, since they knew that this event was repeated a few times and asked me if I had seen a ghost, I just scared it away with my barking. So, even though at the beginning was fun to see them scared, it was not funny to become the official ghost hunter of the family.

As the years passed, my life became more quiet and peaceful every time, little by little I was losing interest in going out to the street, I was losing agility, and something was bothering me, I felt that something was growing inside me and this time were not my sweet puppies who I didn't see any more. The last months of my 15 year of life I started feeling pain, I complained, and I had a tremor in the body that I couldn't control until the pain decreased. No one knew or noticed that something wrong was happening to me, until one morning, before dawn I felt that my time was about to end. The thing that had grown in my tummy hurt so much. I gathered the strength to go with my owners, they were still sleeping. I just wanted to be close to see them for the last time and thank them for all those years that they cared me and shared with me. I arrived with great difficulty to the door, I would have liked to say, "I have to go." "so long then and thank you for loving me, I will carry you in my heart." But it was not possible, my last look was directed to the door that was never opened. There, on the cold ground, they found my body next to the door when they came out.

I think it was very hard for them and they wept over my lifeless body; with deep sorrow and respect I was buried in the garden, as I read in their heart that they wanted me to stay forever. I wanted to comfort them, telling them that it was okay, that there was no pain, no more hunger, or cold, I felt relieved and happy, and I would never forget them; but I couldn't let them know. So, I expect they feel better after my departure and now I only visit them once in a while in their dreams to show how good I am, running between beautiful fields of flowers and playing with some old friends and my puppies who some of them are already with me.

I feel happy and satisfied, because the lessons that I came to teach were well assimilated; they are now a family who learned to overcome adversity and to wait with patience for better times to have hope no matter what the problem is, they also learned tolerance and gratitude. In spite of the years that have passed since I left them, I am still fondly remembered by them.

claudio

Let me introduce myself: Cock-a-doodle-doo!

Sorry!", I forgot that you don't understand my language, so I will speak to you just as you do. After all, how much could a rooster say about his short life? The life of us the feathered creatures is really very short, some of our poor brothers end up in a pot as stew, others rotating well roasted and many others in some other dish, but also cooked. It was a Fortune to not end up in some broth, but death is hopeless for all.

I don't remember how my story starts because I do not have my transition from egg to chicken very clear. My first memories are when we were in some place in a small cage shared by many chicks like me. It was a place full of vendors with thousands of things such as food and all kinds of objects that humans tend to buy to taste or need. We were very crowded, nervous about the hustle and bustle of so many people coming and going from one side to the other in all directions; traders screamers who offered their products to all those who passed; also, those who by carelessness and haste beat our cage without precaution making us almost fall down. Then the curious who came to observe tenderhearted our beauty and finally, the children who without malice but with the rudeness that characterizes them, squeezed us in their small hands while they were melting of tenderness to be able to play with us.

And there we were! waiting to be purchased by whoever

wanted to pay the price. It was uncomfortable to stay there, since it was a long day and they did not give us something to drink or eat just to be presentable, sometimes we felt we were going to faint from hunger and thirst but in general, we resisted. One by one, every day we were taken from the cage and each time we were less the ones that returned.

One day a girl came to see us, was a little girl with a special look. She didn't squeeze us like the others, she saw us tenderly and smiled.

– What is the price of the chicks? She asked the seller.

When he answered, she took some coins that she had brought and give to him. He allowed her to choose the chicks that she would like to have. Among all of them it was me. She put us in a basket that seemed designed especially for us with a lot of care, we were five chicks. We were transported carefully until her home, making a stop in a store of fodder where she bought different kind of food for us. Once she finished, we went home. She seemed a little nervous upon entering, she observed towards all sides and when she was in the garden she freed us. It looked like Paradise! It was a large garden with hundreds of delicious and appetizing insects to taste. We began to explore the new field when suddenly a shout startled us, especially to her:

- WHO GAVE YOU PERMISSION TO BUY CHICKENS????

We ran in all directions scared and chirping:

- DANGER, DANGER! "The end of the world is about" - "Quick, all hide away".

Fortunately, it was not so hard. The end of the world had not come

She intercepted her angry mom and tried to calm her down telling her that she had saved enough to buy and maintain her chicks, she explained to her mom that she had earned the right to have them and raise them and that she would take care of them responsibly; and she did so.

A few weeks later, there was a strange sickness and it was inevitable that one by one, my brothers would begin to sleep and didn't wake any more. I notice how my owner suffered with the loss of every one of them. Finally, she seemed happy that I had healthy and she said:

- "Thank you for staying with me, you are really strong"

Of course, that made me feel very happy and I decided to become her protector as gratitude to her care and love for me.

Little by little I became a handsome cock, she named me Claudio. I had a white and beautiful plumage and gallantry; I also had my own personality and I had reached a big size which is something unusual in the chickens of my species. I think it was due to the good food and good treatment that I received from her.

After a few months the mother said "That chicken is to a best turn, we are going to eat it before it is old and its meat does no longer serve".

My owner simply replied:

- Don't dare to touch it, my rooster is not to eat!!!
- So, what do you think to do with him? It is a rooster, it is to eat isn't it? Asked the mother

To which she responded:

- I just want to have it and care for it, look how beautiful it is! Who told you that you can only have it to eat?

She said it so severely that no one tried to challenge her, not even her own mother.

I was surprised by the great love that she felt for me. So, I decided to become also her protector. But how could a rooster protect a human being? I realized that, despite my size, I had been endowed with some tools that I would use for that purpose, little by little, I developed my skills. When someone knocked on the door, I was ready to defend the house. I watched carefully the visitor, if I felt distrust, I walked away a little to run and attack with my powerful lugs. My peak was my other weapon. Certainly, that worked, was able to ward off the evil-intentioned with kicks and pecks. Sometimes it was necessary to defend my owners and I did it, even when they rebuked her unfairly, I went out in her defense. This made many people think that I was rather different than a common rooster, I behaved like a guardian dog.

The animals are more than just animals, we have the ability to learn what they want to teach us; no matter what language we speak, our understanding is beyond words, we are able to see what cannot be seen with the eyes, we can see the intention of humans, no matter if you are a dog, cat, rooster or cow; we can know if our owners are at risk in the presence of someone who disguise their intentions. We also have the sensitivity to perceive the emotional state of human beings, and we are always there to help them in some way, even if they don't realize it.

Among other things, I became the alarm of my owner. It is a natural gift in us the birds to perceive the first rays of the new day and announce it to all species around. She had to get up with the first rays to attend her activities and she always woke up with the thunderous and terrible sound of the mechanical alarm so I decided to get her up with my sweet song. So, in the morning I sang every day before dawn. It didn't matter if it was cold, hot, or it was raining, I stood at the top of my house to sing.

She always appreciated the wake up in the morning, she told me it was the best that could have someone; For me, it was a pleasure.

The house where we lived was very large, in reality there were two houses which were separated by a garden and a central courtyard. My small owner lived in the last house and I was living next to it. The other house was rented by two families. In the first part, a solitary, anger and bossy grandmother lived, on whom I wanted to use my special character; even on one occasion, I heard her say to my owner's mother that in spite of being a simple rooster, I was very rebellious, it would be best to make a good broth and eat me before I was old. I must confess that I put the feathers up and try always to be alert for not letting me cook for that grandmother without a heart.

The other part of the house was occupied by a young family that had two little children. I had no problem with them, except that sometimes they liked to pluck me the feathers. It was really horrible and painful for me, so in order to avoid it, I rushed around them all over the yard to their home and that was enough for not coming back out of the house of course, this was not funny for their mother and she began to look at me with anger.

At the end, for all those who knew me, I listened to say that I was a dog dressed as a rooster because no one had known a rooster with such behavior. Especially when I came to protect my sweet owner. No one explained my strange behavior, there was nothing strange on it. It was simple correspondence and gratitude for the love and protection I received. As you surely Know in the animal kingdom we are faithful unto death.

Therefore, we mutually care each other my owner and me all the time. I Enjoyed a life of peace and joy by her side, I went out to receive her when she arrived at home and together we spent many happy hours because she always had some time to play with me. It was always also nice to see the arrival of a new day, because for us the animals one day is not the same to the previous one; that is why I sang with joy, all the sunrises.

My life was very brief, perhaps a couple of years, maybe

a little bit more. But the most important thing is that I have been lived intensely every moment without worrying about what will happen next. At least that is the purpose for us the animals and in some way is what we have to teach to humans.

One day someone got tired of my excessive protection to the family and decided to put an end. One night near my house when my owner was sleeping, I found a container with a delicious snack that I decided to eat innocently and without distrust. I finished all the content that had been sprayed with a powerful poison which, after a few moments started to take effect: I felt an intense pain in the entrails, that I felt I was burning like fire. I tried to reach to my house and I thought that resting I would feel better. The deep sleep of death surprised me and did not allow me to receive the new day with my singing. My young owner noticed my absence at dawn and ran to see what was wrong with me, finding my body cold and lifeless. Her pain was very large, crying and asking for justice for such cruel murder. She wondered what kind of heart could be so cruel to commit such an act. She hugged me and said goodbye to me I was buried in the garden and wishing that I was ok, in calm and happy I also heard her prayer to soften those hard hearts that hurt so many defenseless beings of this world. Thus, ends the story of Claudio, full of joy, love, gratitude and not very common. Although I had a tragic outcome, I decide to take the best part, which made me live in the fond memory of who loved me.

giacomo

Hello, my name is or call me Giacomo. This name was given to me because I had so much sensitivity as Giacomo Puccini, the well-known Italian Musician. I was the most amazing German Shepherd and exceptional according to my owner that I'll call my mom in this story. Why I call her like this?" because that was for me while I lived.

My story begins in the house of a family like any other who likes to have pets. In this case, they had a couple of German Shepherds which were my parents. I was born in a litter of seven healthy and strong puppies. First, we were a bit awkward as all the puppies but little by little we were learning to move and began the exploration of the large yard where we lived. To be realistic and mature we became more bold and playful. We also began to develop the taste to try other things. I remember that the family spent part of their time to preparing and selling BBQ facilities for social events. They spent long hours preparing it and baking in a brick oven especially designed for this. The next day, the buyers went to collect their food. I still remember the delicious aroma coming out when they uncovered the oven to remove the cooked meat, that delicious meat almost finished with my life.

It happened that, with just four weeks of age, my brothers and I were exploring as always, the front yard. Suddenly we felt attracted by the delicious smell permeated in the leaves of agave of the flesh that, a few hours ago had just turned in. You have to know that the meat is cooked wrapped in the leaves inside the oven.

Our owners were so busy with other tasks that they didn't realize that. They had forgotten to discard the leaves and remove them from our reach. So innocently we went to taste them attracted by the smell.

We ate a little of those leaves and it did not last long before the symptoms of a terrible diarrhea began to manifest in all of us. We all the puppies started almost simultaneously with the diarrhea and it did not stop until we were empty from our stomachs. After this, the dehydration started and we were seriously ill, causing us to lose weight immediately. It took a long time to our owners to realize about our situation and what had caused it. As fast as possible, they took us to the doctor, who attended to us immediately trying to save our lives. The doctor did all the necessary emergency cares to stop the disease of our small bodies. I have to confess that my life could have ended there, with just five weeks of age, without ever having known more of the world and life but my destination was different from most of my brothers who after several days of intense struggle to live, some of them lost the battle. I was one of the only three survivors. However, I want to point out that there was less hope that we could be alive. The disease ended with my body mass, my small figure was reduced to a skeletal and stunted body, because my damaged stomach was reluctant to withhold food that they made me eat with difficulty. I looked like a piece of skin with bones, very unattractive to the sight of a purchaser of a genuine German Shepherd. Given the circumstances our owners began their search for buyers of dogs. The fear that we might die and the tiredness to keep on caring, made them decide to offer us on sale the puppies that were left.

My mom was the first to be called to choose a puppy. They told her to go as soon as possible, as there were plenty to choose from. I remember when she came to choose her puppy, my brothers began to twirl around. And me? I had no strength to get out of my uncomfortable place, so I limited myself to observe her choice with a certain sadness, due to my circumstances the probability of being chosen was almost zero.

I saw how she looked with enthusiasm to my brothers and all of a sudden, my owner asked:

- And well, what do you say? Have you already chosen one?

She was still carefully watching and she was very analytical and intuitive. She didn't answer instead she directed her look to the corner where I was, her look was so deep that I felt a little sorrow for my condition. She reached out and carefully took me between her hands and stared at me. It was a strange connection that we both felt when our eyes crossed for a few moments. Immediately, she asked:

- How much is the small one?

My owner replied with amazement and a certain sentence:

- I can't sell that one, sorry, you better choose another one.

The girl insisted:

- Why not? Is it already booked for someone else?

To which she answered timidly:

- It is not right for you, he will die. "I have already told you what happened to them. The truth is that I don't think that he will live for a long time, because many days have passed and cannot be relieved. -Holds nothing piece of food, he only survives with a bit of serum. - Seriously, choose another one!

The girl immediately responded calmly and firmly:

- I don't want another one, I love this! I'll take him right now!
- You really don't! The woman replied. - Definitively is not for you, you will lose your money, the puppy will die!
- I assume the risk, -replied the girl- I think will be worth it! don't worry, there will be no claim on my part.
- But….
- No buts! she said to the woman
- It's good! - The woman replied- …and I don't want to be unfair or to say "I told you so", to do this, I won't take the payment, the puppy is yours, just take it.

The girl seriously replied:

– Why shouldn't I pay? He is worth as much as the others…

The woman was already quite nervous and surprised at the same time and she answered:

– "Are you crazy? How is going to be worth the same a healthy puppy that one dying? I'm sure that he will die in less than two days!!! and I don't want to self-reproach for not doing the right thing, I insist! It was given to you, and I will not accept a No!

The girl paused for a moment and said:

– It's good! If you insist, I will take your offer. I only hope that after not to regret….

The woman answered:

– Believe Me I will not.

And with no more to say, the girl pulled out a small canvas fabric and wrapped it carefully, hugged him and left.

On the way home, she kept looking at me and she said: - don't die! You 'll stay with me because I love you very much and will take care of you always.

These were the magic words that begin my recovery. With her care and love, I began to feel much better, she feed me

40

very well and with the best that she could get. With patience I was fed, cleaned up and sought my comfort in my rest. For my side I decided to comply with the treatment, I would stay by her side!

A month after my arrival in my new home, I was much better: I had gained weight, my fur began to change, regain your strength and my countenance improved markedly, even began to play a bit with my mom who always reserved a time for me.

In the house lived also a female of my same species called Dolly, she belonged to the sister of my mom, and was very playful and excellent guardian. She used to do some pranks that were not well seen by the family like to pull the clothes of the drying racks, taking out the trash and break area rugs. This of course make her to win numerous punishments and a lick. In this regard, I am grateful to my mommy that in spite of my antics never hurt me and nor allow others to do. In the end, we share the same courtyard and the same house, Dolly became my playmate. At the beginning, I was very patient, for I was very small and a little clumsy, but after we did good dumbbell we got on very well together.

A few months later, there was a lot of agitation and movement at home; because they were going to initiate the construction of a house in which to live, the reason was that my mom would marry later with my future Dad. I liked him a lot, he was a good person and he also played with me when he visited her. Thus, began with the construction and everything was uproar, and with much disorder at the workers were entering and leaving tools, and materials for construction.

This new situation made us feel very nervous because we saw a lot of unknown people all days. Dolly barked incessantly, while I wanted to play with everything they had. The family then decided to protect us making a little yard with wire mesh to keep us inside it during the day. They were working all the afternoon and they didn't let us leave but when they finished and left, the fun began. I spent the night exploring the things that were brought, the holes that were made, the mountains of material left. I could not say what was my favorite activity, a few times I had fun digging holes in the sand, others biting a few funny shoes used by the workers, or throwing them in the large holes that they had made to build the foundations of the house, we also tried to find the use to all those strange tools that they left there. At the end of the day, there was so much to be done.... So, all days after sunset I spent long hours in these issues. Dolly was a little bit afraid; I remember the fear that she felt crossing the narrow planks placed to cross over the large holes. You could say that her legs were shaking once she stood there, in spite of the panic for falling down I encouraged her to continue by showing her how to do it, I was in front of her, to give her a gentle nudge but she went back. Anyways, she never overcame her fear; especially in one of those times, when I was showing at her how easy it was to cross, the planks began to move under my legs, did not want to walk on the edge and I did it the plank turned making me turn down. My reflex was to hold me with my two front legs hugging from the table, but my weight finally overcame and I fell down into the hole. It was very funny! Although it wasn't for Dolly who looked at me terrified.

As the circumstances did not permit it (for my good fortune) my owners weren't able to give me a bath for a while, so I enjoyed giving me my own baths of earth. It was fascinating to dig holes in the earth mounds, then I buried myself in them. I think I was the happiest puppy in the world than any dog would be, since these works lasted almost one year.

The time passed, and I became a big, strong and healthy German Shepherd. My mom was proud of me. There were also some changes at home. Now my dad was with us, and in a small apartment next door, the grandmother was installed, and I had fun making her some little jokes.

A good day, Dolly and I became parents. It was a strange experience, because all of a sudden, she didn't want me to come closer, she was very irritable and she stopped playing with me. Six beautiful and healthy puppies were born. The first few days, Dolly cared for them feeding and cleaning them; but as they began to grow up and to leave the nest, she was got tired of these tasks, she delegated to me that responsibility. I was overseeing the small puppies and I had to clean and play with them but when they were hungry and cried without ceasing, I had no more than ask for help to Dolly, since I had no way to relieve their ferocious appetite.

When they were older, they were adopted by different families who were interested in them, so one by one they went to a new home and everything was back to normal. I returned to make jokes to grandmother, I sometimes went without being seen to her house and I pulled out her slippers to hide them in my house; it's a shame that when I realized it, it was just fun. Also, I sometimes ran in the morning because I went quietly under her bed while she was still sleeping, then I began to move underneath and pushed it a little bit, she was so superstitious that she just jumped immediately from the bed thinking that it was a ghost that agitated her bed, she ran by saying that her bed was haunted.

Other days the grandmother played pretending that I couldn't get my food and I would not be permitted, I hugged my plate very strong with my two front legs and she laughed for my reaction.

Everything was perfect until my parents wanted to give me a bath. What a horror! They were running behind me to trap me and I ran until the madness, they had to tie me to a safe place and they didn't let me go. Watching myself in such a hard situation I started emitting a lot of pitiful cries to convince them not to bath. After a while, I resigned myself because I was finally given a bath. I wanted it to end, the water was cold and it was terrible but as soon as I was released I ran in terror shaking the water.

I don't know why they insisted on bathing me with water if the earth was healthier and delicious.

Some time passed and Dolly and me were parents a couple of times more. The dynamic was always the same. Dolly rested while I was crazy caring for my puppies. When things are out of control and all cried at the same time, I just also cried with them because I didn't know what to do. Everybody seemed funny about my role of the pup's nanny.

A couple of months later, my parents also had a baby, they gave a feast to celebrate the arrival of the little one. Here there was a very painful and important event in my life and I believe that in the whole family.

The celebration would be in the great courtyard of the house, so they brough some tables and chairs for the guests, it was not very appropriate that they allowed us to stay there, not for bad behavior, but for any inconvenience to the guests because our size could a certain fear in people. For this reason, they decided to take us to the terrace of the house to stay there during the event. It was not bad because it was like another backyard, and also have our little house and enough water and food.

There we stayed until it was over, the family was very busy collecting and sorting all over again. The men came out to deliver the chairs and tables they had rented and only women were at home. My dear Dolly began to be impatient, as she was quite restless she wanted to go back to our yard. Seeing that no one was coming to get us out, she began to seek a way out. There was a cube of ventilation from the roof to the main floor, which had been covered for our safety with some sheets. Dolly, impatient, sought to move to the cube standing on the blades. It didn't take a long time and her weight was very similar to a child of 7 or 8 years of age, so the sheets sank letting it fall into space.

The following moments were the most terrible and painful

for all. First, we heard the scream of pain from my dear Dolly falling to the ground. Later, all the women that were in the courtyard cried very nervous knowing that something terrible had happened. Suddenly I heard them crying, shouting and someone calling Dad by telephone and those who were outside came immediately as fast as they could, they got Dolly into a car very carefully, and went to the hospital.

My Dolly, did not return. I just saw my dad who sounded like a sea of tears saying that Dolly died in his arms shortly before arriving at the hospital. There was nothing to do. He was crying and blamed himself for the bad fortune of Dolly, but who would know? Who would have though that Dolly was going to climb up there? She was more fearful than me to cross by a table on a hole. It was incredible and terrible at the same time!

Little by little the spirits and the faults calmed down and we all started to get used to her absence. I missed playing with her, her company, and even when she was angry with me and I barked because she did not want to play with me. I was a little sad and lonely.

Time passed and I found myself alone, I was looking for new ways to play and it didn't happen, it was so boring. Remember that I like children because I felt that we somehow resemble each other. The problem is that sometimes my size caused them fear.

On one occasion, somebody left the door open I don't know why. I peeked timidly, I had almost never gone out to the street. All of a sudden, some children were playing happily on the street. Immediately, and without thinking I ran toward them to join in the game; but when they saw me coming so abruptly towards them, they ran away screaming:

- HEEEELP! THE DOG REACHES US! AAAAAH!

Realizing that they were scared, I preferred to go back not to get into trouble; so, I turned around and went back towards the house. But Oh mistake! without wanting, I mistook the door of my house with the neighbor's one which also was open, and without paying attention, I got in. There was a boy standing there, and when he saw me coming, he began to shout frightened:

- HEEEELP! A BIG DOG HAS JUST COME IN!

Oh no! I thought, here we go again! With fear I ran back into the street, I stood a moment looking towards all sides, when suddenly I heard the voice of my mother saying to me:

- Hey Giaco! What are you doing in the street?, What happened?

Happy to see her and a little ashamed for have been lost practically at the door of the street, I came into the house.

Other times they had very nice birthday parties, there were tons of sweets that fell down from the piñatas and I always sought to earn some, I also tried to get a piece of piñata which I considered "My Trophy".

Time after, I also came back to do my usual jokes to grandmother with her shoes or slippers, but she never scolds me for that; on the contrary, I felt she had some affection for me because she sometimes gave me some candy or extra food and went to talk with me. I think that we became good friends; so much, that when she died, again I felt sad and I sat down in front of her door for some time missing her.

A few months after the departure of the grandmother, my parents also moved to a small apartment in the city in which there was not enough space for me. So, I was left at home with other relatives. Although I was not alone, I felt deeply sad when they left. Although my mom explained to me that it was necessary to move and that it was very bad not to take me, she also promised not to abandon me and go to see me frequently. They fulfilled their promise, and frequently they went to the house, playing with me and pampered. It gave me so much joy when they arrived, and one of those times, I couldn't contain the emotion and I made such an effort that from my muzzle came out strong and clear the word "MAMMA". All of them were paralyzed to hear me speak, from the biggest to the smallest of the family. She was the only one who could react and told me:

- Giaco, did you call me Mamma?
- Oh, my little one, I love you! And of course, I am your mom! You're my naughty boy!

No one came out of the astonishment and wondered:

- Did he say mom?
- Yes, I did it!

The years were still going on and I became very old, I no longer ran and jumped as well, My feet hurt when I climbed the stairs, I lost some teeth and I could no longer eat the same even with the change of food that they gave me. My mom was visiting and reminding me how much she loved me but seeing that every time my condition got worst again, sad; I listened to her say she didn't want me to die, so I clung to life, although each time it cost me more to do so.

One day I got sick and they came for me to take me to the doctor, despite my size, dad was carrying me so that I wouldn't hurt myself because at that time, I was very weak. The doctor gave me some medicine, but my body was already very old and tired. They accepted my situation and my mom told me that I did not have to suffer anymore. She told me that she loved me and thanked me for coming to brighten their lives and I didn't have to stay if I could no longer do so. She said that they always would love me and that I would live in their heart and I could leave whenever I wanted.

I stayed only a few more days, just the time to leave a special gift for them. After that, one day early in the morning while I was sleeping I died in calm and at peace.

They embraced and wept me, and they also told me not to worry, that everything would be fine and that I would feel free and happy because I will always be loved. After a few days, between tears and surprise they discovered my gift for them: on a wall, with my own legs, scratching, I drew in the plaster a small portrait of myself that I left to remember me; I know that it still remains in that wall. They say it is the memory of the artist Giacomo, an artist whose sensitivity was able to express outstandingly.

thumbelina

Hello everyone, my name is Thumbelina, and I am really small, not as the character in the previous story but I am too small. I was born among 7 brothers of whom I was the smaller in size. Four weeks after birth I was adopted. My sisters and brothers were very excited, but I felt a little upset and nervous.

One day in the evening came the family who wanted to adopt. They brought their two children to choose the puppy that like them the most, the boys looked at us, talked and watched us one by one, until they finally chose me. They said that my gaze was charmingly tender and sweet. Thus, after listening to a series of instructions to feed me and take care of me, my new owners were recognized by me as my parents and they came out of the house with me in their arms. The girl radiated happiness and thanked their parents for the gift that had been me. Apparently, she had been asking to have a puppy for a long time, precisely just like my race and finally her wish was granted.

When we arrive to my new house, Immediately my sister Norah looked for something that help me feel better to be comfortable. She brought a warm blanket and in a little box she prepared a cozy bed, she also put containers with a little bit of food and milk. They received me with so much love and warmth, which took no time for me to feel good in my new family and home.

The first few weeks, I was not allowed to leave outside because I was still too small to be vaccinated and they did want me to get sick. When the time came, they took me to the doctor and to give me everything I needed to be healthy. They also initiated the delicious baths with warm water in the bathroom sink; for being so small, it was the perfect jacuzzi for me.

My family attended me very well and gave me love and respect, because they considered that the animals also deserve to be respected as every living being. They were respectful to the plants, animals, insects, trees and any being that might have life. I was fortunate to find a family like mine. That's why my life was really good and pleasant.

My training to educate me in some important habits for humans began soon after I arrived. I learned to make my needs in a specific place they appointed when I couldn't get out. I also have a place to eat and another to relax or sleep during the day. But there were some things that they did not know how to check on me, for it is inherent in the dogs of my race, I am very restless and playful.

I remember one time: I went to the closet and took one of the Dad's shoes, I began to chew it because I tasted and felt pretty good. Of course, I hide it for a few days to continue enjoying it. As he had been asking everyone if somebody had seen his shoe, the mom got worried and began the search until she found it. When she found she said scary:

- Holy God, Thumbelina! Daddy is going to hang you up when he sees what you did to his favorite shoe.

But it didn't happen, I do not deny that when she showed the shoe to Dad made a face of horror at the terrible state it was in. Besides, that shoe had not been the only one I had also chewed one of the children's, some clothes and some toys. So, then he said:

- You're a little naughty Thumbelina! You broke one of my favorite shoes! All this is why you have to take a canine training course to educate you.
- Oh, oh! - I thought - What does that exactly mean?

When it was time to start. Dad found a dog trainer who liked to use the method of the obedience training without punishment; even though I felt very nervous and worried. I didn't know what I was going to do, I was afraid, just like children on their first day of classes.

I was taken to the training camp and I met the coach. He was very sensitive with the animals. On that first day I was watched all the time, and I was very shy, I became even more nervous and I looked for shelter with my family, but that didn't bother him at all, On the contrary, he said that to have a good bond among us, it would be very easy for them to train me while he would be just the guide.

The training was more than nice because all the time I had awards so I behaved very well to receive many rewards. The coach was very surprised by my performance and my family even more. Everything turned out very well, and in a short time I had learned basic rules of behavior very easily. So, I stopped making mischief and I became more obedient, you do not have to be so smart to know what is really right and good for you: If you do well, there will be prize; if you don't do it, there will not be one. So, I decided to behave well to have those delicious bites of turkey sausage. Simply delicious!

As I said before, I learned many things in the training but my restless nature prevailed. I like running, chasing rodents, insects, and some cats, playing with balls and balloons, I also like playing with stuffed animals and run with children. My family says I'm as another girl in the house: greedy, playful, pamper and also dramatic.

Although I am only two years my life is full of adventures, most of them funny. I will tell you about some of them, I should clarify that some are before the trainings and other later.

One morning we went out for a walk, Norah was holding me. Of course, I was very excited and euphoric as always when we went out; we walked down a small street when I suddenly let go of my rope and I ran desperately towards the park where they played with me. I had not reached my maximum height yet so I was even smaller, then a car suddenly came out I don't know where from, when I was running to the middle of the street. Norah was already running after me, but it was a long distance from each other, was very difficult to reach me, when she saw the car, she used a sign language and shouted at the driver to stop but apparently, he did not hear or did not understand, so the car continued running and it did not stop. When I saw him approaching me I only jumped in the middle of the street and the poor Norah launched a cry when the car was over me. Fortunately, I remained in the middle and the car did not make me any harm. She ran as fast as she could towards the place I was and hugged me while she wondered if I was okay. What a shock! I think if I had moved I would not be telling more adventures.

Another day we went with a friend who lives next door, she was very nice and gentle with animals, she always cared for and protected them, her name is Lisa and we became good friends. In the place where she lives there is a little park. Lisa and my Mom like to stay there sometimes to talk while the kids and me have a lot of fun. They taught me to walk up and down the slide, get in the swing and also in another games; I also like to participate with them in volleyball, basketball and soccer. Although I am small, I always catch the ball.

At the beginning, I didn't like cats because sometimes when I wanted to greet them, they looked very aggressive while they showed their sharp-edged nails and they were shouting too:

– GET OUT OF HERE, DON'T BOTHER ME!!!

So, I decided not to get closer to them, but they also put me on guard if they wanted to attack.

In the place where Lisa lives there were several cats. Although they didn't belong to her, she cared for and fed them. In addition, she liked to play and talk with them. Lisa helped me to reconciled with them, she introduced me with one cat called Pummy, very noble and gentle. She taught us to greet bumping noses and live together in harmony. So, the visits to Lisa's home were very frequent, I like going to visit her because I always had a good piece of chicken for me and she was extremely loving and gentle. There was also her mother Mrs. Esther who lives with her and always received me affectionately. Also, I did some antics, one day I made pis in her bedroom, so I was ashamed and I hide it under a rug; or when they gave me a friendly mouse toy that it liked me so much and I derailed it when I was playing with it.

On one occasion, my family had to leave out of the city and they could not take me so Lisa was very kind and offered to take care of me. Although I missed my family a lot, Lisa and her Mom made me feel like home. Nowadays, I don't see them but always remember them as my great friends and I hope to see them once more.

One day, my Mom was cooking some delicious breaded chicken, the smell was nice but obviously it was not part of my menu. Literally my mouth was drooling and asked insistently for a little piece to taste but I was not successful. I waited until Mom went to pick up the kids from school. Then I was thinking in the best way to take one of those from the stove where the plate was on. When I started the almost impossible mission to catch a fillet; I looked for something to help me up or drive to jump, but with my size it was very difficult to reach that height. Since I found nothing, I tested my legs, I started by making small jumps and every time I tried to get higher; with difficulty and scope in the next hop I hold it to help me up completely. When I did it, I thought that no one would notice if I took only one piece but then I could not resist the temptation to eat one more... and another... and another... until my belly was near to exploit if I ate a little bit more, with the heaviness of my stomach I fell down and as soon as I could get up, literally, I felt that everything that I ate was going to get out, and it was not for less.

When Mom arrived with the children I wasn't able to hide, I was lying on my bed belly up and unable to move. I believe that the indigestion saved me from the reprimand because I was really bad, so much that they had to massage my tummy with an oil for a couple of days to recover. A few days passed so I could go back to eat.

The younger brother called Demian, spend many hours playing with his legos because he loves them. I started to interested in those small pieces which were converted in rockets, boats, ships and platforms, the bad thing is that I wasn't interested in playing, but in chew and eating them. They told me that if I continued eating legos I will lay ill, and it didn't take a long time to happen. Once I think I ate many legos, but that was not the worst, one of the small parts were stuck in my throat and it hurt me so much that I couldn't breathe very well. I began to ask for help and when they discovered that I had something in my throat, I was taken immediately to the vet. I always avoided to go to that place because I couldn't stand the shots. I had a lot of pain in the throat. I couldn't breathe very well and I also I was very nervous, therefore I didn't let her to check me. The doctor had to give me a sedative to calm me down but it didn't work, I defended myself as a cat face up and she could not find the stuck object. Seeing my poor cooperation in the consultation, the doctor decided to give me some anesthesia that gave me more dread, I didn't want to fall asleep and wake up and see my family; they could not believe that with a sedative and anesthetic I could continue fighting to prevent to be checked. The sedative finally won, and the doctor tried to remove the object of my throat. She also explored my stomach and said that I probably had eaten more than one lego, so she gave me a medicine to dispose it. When I returned home, I was still numb, I was happy to came back but I could not express it. When Norah saw me, she was scared, but mom explained that everything was fine, and I would wake up soon. I spent that night very well because they took care of me and let me sleep in the bed with them. I love to sleep on the bed! After a couple of days when I went to the restroom to make poop I expelled so many Legos to build a small toy. I couldn't believe the number of legos which were in my belly!

Another small incident was when I started playing in the
skating rink. As I had already learned to jump up to the stove,
one day without wanting to spill the oil bottle while I was

looking for something to eat, the oil fell down on the kitchen floor and when I came down to inspect, it was the liquid that fell, I felt how my small legs slid almost by themselves on the floor. Then I discovered the skating rink! I spent a long-time skating on the floor of the kitchen, the dining room and in the living room as well. Although it was fun, I was exhausted after doing it; so, I was ready to go to sleep. When they got back to the house, they nearly fell off with the oil spilt and scattered everywhere. Then, they almost had an attack when they discovered that all the floors were fully greased. I remember the time it took mom to degrease all floors....

I also remember another day in which they let me go to leave the kids to school; I was really excited, especially because there were so many children. I wanted to run and play with them, but I was tied to my leash for safety. Mom stopped inside the school to talk with teachers and I only wanted to explore the whole place. I was able to release from my leash and I ran in the yard to inspect everything I could see. Suddenly, mom began to call me and ask for help to someone to stop me. I broke out and many people were chasing me to catch me such as the teachers, the monitoring staff and some children but I am faster than lightning and I always managed to avoid them. I started feeling nervous because everybody wanted to catch me so noted the door was still open and I ran towards it. The person who was watching tried to stop me closing the door but she was about to crush me or split me in two so she opened the door again and without thinking twice I continued with my fabulous flight. I ran toward the street but was still full of cars that were arriving to leave children. I also saw many moms who were walking besides the staff controlling the transit. When I arrived to the middle of the street I heard that everybody shouted:

- ¡¡¡A PUPPY!!!
WATCH UP!!!!!

And then mom ran out of the school shouting:

– PLEASE, STOP THE CARS!!!!

Immediately everybody shouts to signal the cars to stop. There were also some people trying to surround me to catch me. Somebody crossed on the street to prevent the cars to move while mom was running towards me to see if I was okay. While all this was happening, I had a panic attack that left me paralyzed in the middle of the street and I just stayed there, rolled up, trembling like jelly and looking with a face of terror everything that happened. Seconds later, I got out of my traumatic shock when I saw mom coming to me and embraced me asking me if I was fine. I WAS SAVED! what a relief!

I honestly felt a little embarrassed for having caused such chaos and for giving such a tremendous shock to the world, especially to mom who looked noticeably nervous and embarrassed with all the people involved whom she thanked them for their help.

Another day, Demian was coloring with crayons. For some reason he had not keep their crayons and then they left. I began to explore these new things, I sniff a little and in fact, I liked the smell so I decided to taste a few pieces that I found. Of course, when they arrived they realized were missing many crayons. Les a little worried what might happen as an effect, but when they read on the packaging, the legend of "Non- toxic" they calmed down and decided to wait until the following day to see what happened.

I felt nothing strange on my body, except for wanting to go to make poop and I felt I should go fast. After having released my gut Norah was ready to clean and suddenly shouted:

-   OH, MY GOD!!! LOOK AT WHAT THUMBELINA
    HAS DONE!!!

We all ran where I had done certain things and discovered a great mountain of poop painted in multiple colors. Everybody was watching with amazement and Norah said:

-   WOWWW THUMBELINA, YOU'RE A GREAT
    ARTIST!!!
-   ¡LOOK AT YOUR MASTERPIECE!

I looked at her with a face of: are you kidding? I felt a little embarrassed…

Time after, a great change for the family was about to happen. They were planning a change in all senses. We had to move to another city, in another country, with another culture and with other customs. The arrangements began months before we left. The reason was that Dad got a new job and he had to take it right away. I knew that we were going to depart a few months later and Mom put everything in order to be able to go. I still don't understand why people change from one job to another and then live in a different place. The only thing I could do was wait patiently.

Finally, the day arrived, I hated going in the trip cage because I really can't move, eat, or go to the restroom among other things. The van that took us to the airport was full with suitcases, bags, a Mom, two kids and a little sweet dog (me).

I Could summarize you the trip as totally terrible especially for me who was locked up, there was a delay in the first flight and to top it off, we missed the connecting flight. We had to spend the night in a hotel until the next day to take another flight. After spending more than 10 hours in my cage, when Mom took me out in the hotel, I no longer felt my legs, I wanted to walk but I was numb and I could not stand up. Little by little I regained mobility and my family was worried and they gave me some food and water instantly. Once I was recovered I jumped happily from one bed to another and I explored the room to see if I could find something interesting or some delicious candy. We slept almost instantly because everybody was exhausted. Early the next day, we left again to take the next flight, in a few hours we were with Dad who was waiting for us. I was happy to see him again, and express my happiness skipping without stopping on his legs.

Soon we were in the new home, everything was very different, even the weather. I felt ease but I had to start to explorer the new ground as soon as possible. I was taken to the forest that was behind the house, it was fantastic! There was a lot of land where to scratch, and a space to run, a creek to get wet because it was very hot, and the best: Squirrels! Hundreds of these for hunting, as you know, the instinct of my race is to hunt rodents of all kinds.

Everything was perfect, there was a park very close where I could play on the slide and it was hilarious. Only one thing that scared me were my canine companions who were very erratic to get to know me and introduced because so much euphoria sometimes scared me, so I marked my territory to keep them away a little.

I love to run and catch the ball or play frisbee and what I love more than any other thing is to hunt squirrels, especially because one day one of them laughed at me. We went to walk in the forest when suddenly a little squirrel came out of its burrow running towards the nearest tree. I came out as an arrow following it as soon as I could see it but escaped from me because i couldn't upload more to the tree where it had climbed, I tried to climb only a few feet by the impulse and after, I felt down belly up. I decided not to let it go, I was lurking out there without leaving a lot, but I felt that the small rodent was very attentive to all my movements. In fact, minutes later it went back quietly to its lair, I was very pending to run after her. Again, I was about to reach it before I could climb the tree; I tried again climb behind her when the silly squirrel slipped from the trunk and fell right into+ my snout that I had wide open because I was barking. Everything happened in fraction of seconds, I was not able to react because of her furry tail, I was choking myself while she did not lose a single second of time she jumped again to the tree to escape from my jaws while I did not stop coughing for the itching that left her hairs in my throat. As soon as I recover, I started barking furiously and she looked at me mockingly from the branch of a tree. I could not believe or accept that this little rodent made fun of that way of me. It was outrageous!

As you can imagine, I want to clean my honor capturing one of those squirrels. I hope to do it someday.

The summer is ending, and it is really fascinating to see

how everything changes in every season of the year. It is strange to go out into the forest and feel the crunch of the leaves under my feet every time I walk it, is really fun, it makes me want to jump on it. Norah always says that I look like grasshoppers because I am jumping and jumping all the time, but I love it, especially because I can jump and run without stopping without suffocating and falling almost fainted for the searing heat of the summer I sometimes have to jump into the river to calm down and giving myself a refreshing dip. The fall is rather cool, not too hot or too cold, you can spend more time outside and it is perfect for Halloween. You have to know that I love Halloween because I like to go out disguised with the children to ask for sweets. It is not very common for dogs to be transformed, so that makes me earn my own treats.

I know, I am a charm! And if we add my dreamy look, no

one can resist giving me candy or food. Some family friends always tell me:

- Oh, my God! With those sweet eyes I can give you all my food.

And it works! When I want something that they are eating, I just crave, enough to lay my dreamer eyes and they give me some food right away. It is a good trick, I have always said that we have to exploit our virtues.

Now comes the cold winter. For all the heavens! I am freezing! I believe that in reality I don't like the idea of going out to the forest and the park. Sometimes I prefer to stay at home doing other interesting things. For example, the other day in which all went to their activities, and I was very bored, I decided to turn on the TV and watch my favorite program. I sat comfortably on the couch between the warm cushions and I was enjoying my program when suddenly mom came back, she was trying to find me when she looked at me watching tv! and I thought:

– Oh, oh, I think I have already been discovered!

Mom had a face of impressive awe. She could not believe that I was watching TV. She told everybody she couldn't believe it at all. How would it be possible for a dog to turn on the TV to watch her favorite program? Yes, definitely the dogs can do some things that humans do not believe that we can do.

In another single day, Dad left his computer on the desk and I decided to see what was on that device in which he spent long hours working. On that screen, I saw many strange symbols that I could not decipher, then I saw a tablet with many squares and many characters in each one; I decided to play it and suddenly when I was typing something happened on the screen, many things moved at great speed. I didn't know what I had done, but I felt proud of having done so. The problem was when Dad came to his computer:

– WHO WAS PLAYING ON MY COMPUTER? WHO DELETED ALL MY WORK???

I thought: Oh, Oh! I think I had better not show up out there....

It started snowing and everyone was very excited for that, I had no idea what it was until I went to play outside. It was the strangest and freezing sensation I had ever felt. I was put on the snow and I began to sink slowly, it scared me a little bit so my reaction was to run but it didn't work because every time I tried to move from one place to another was the same, I was still sinking. I understood that it was frozen, the snow was so soft that you could sink. It took me a few minutes to understand. After that time, I walked again as grasshoppers leaping up to sink everywhere, I was also pleased to try it and I liked it. In fact, I ate a little bit. Suddenly, I felt a blow of ice on my face: the children were starting a war of snowballs against their parents and against me too. It was very funny! Everybody running towards all sides dodging frozen balls. At the end, we were all covered in snow, especially me because when I jumped I sank and my fur was completely white.

Dad went quickly to get a sled and we went to a small slope to slide down. The first were the children, then Dad joined, after him was Mom's turn and finally I had to get on with them. I didn't think it was so incredibly funny to slide on the snow. I just loved it!

All kind of things happen every day of my life, as you will see there is nothing boring or ordinary and I even don't know how long or short it may be but I am determined to live it happy and fully with my family. In the meantime, I will continue enjoying all the good things that I have with gratitude and attitude.

I will keep on teaching my family to enjoy every moment, to live in the here and now; to be tolerant and patient in spite of the circumstances such as the whole day I spent between aircraft and airports without any complaint. I would also like to keep teaching to enjoy the simple things and always have a positive attitude, to live the life without complications and finally never stop being children, tto keep alive our inner child.

I hope later I can continue telling you more adventures that I have lived and experienced throughout my existence. Until then!

tips for caring and making your pet happy

1. When you go to get a pet be sure that is adopted and not purchased. There are hundreds of them hoping to find a home with a loving family that loves them truly.

2. Once you have found your ideal pet, you have to take it to a medical evaluation to rule out any health problem that could have and receive the necessary vaccinations to stay healthy. It is also necessary to deworm it periodically for its well-being and of the whole family too.

3. Feed it always with adequate food recommended preferably by your veterinarian because sometimes what could be good and very healthy for us the humans, it could be extremely harmful for them and sometimes lethal, as in the case of grapes and raisins especially for dogs. This innocent healthy fruit and candy could kill them. So, get well informed about the things that

can harm your pet before you share them with. Food is one of the key points to prolong the life of your pet.

4. If your pet is a female, decide on time if you want puppies from her. If so, look for homes with loving people to take them up for adoption. If you decide that this is not the case, talk to your veterinarian for advice on the best way to prevent the reproduction, also talk about the long-term risks in your pet. Remember that between races, the risks may vary.

5. No matter in what neighborhood, colony, city or country you live, for any reason, don't let your pet go out in the street alone without supervision of someone because it could have an accident, get lost, be exposed to catch any illness or eat something that may be harm or poison.

6. If you are still small and you want to stroll. It could be dangerous for you and your pet. Never go out with an adult person.

7. Interact with your pet, they are so intelligent, they love to spend time and love to play with you, never ignore it because that causes them a lot of sadness on the other hand, be with them and embrace them, it always helps us to relieve stress, sadness, anger or any

other negative emotion that affects our mood, it is extraordinarily relaxing and comforting. Remember the girl who took refuge with Sparky when she felt forgotten and replaced; of course, your pet should not breastfeed, but a hug will make you feel much better if you need it.

8. Talk to them when you are together, you will be surprised to discover how they find a way to respond, they are excellent confidents and they know how to listen to you.

9. Invite them to your exercise routines outside, you always hold the step and you 'll be accompanied. Besides, both of you will be benefited.

10. If you decide to give training, be yourself who train it. Look for a coach that only guides you in what to teach it and how to do it. If you want your pet to obey it must be you who has to train it because the dogs create a strong link with their coach, so it is best that you create that bond and your pet will obey you. Also choose a coach who teaches with the method of "reward for obedience" instead of "punishment for disobedience." In this way you will create the bond and stronger protection of your pet towards you.

11. Express and let them know how much you love them. They will find a way to let you know that he loves you too.

12. Talk to them with love and respect their dignity, they also have it and they are humiliated when you talk of a rude or derogatory way and if there is any kind of batter it is worse. This form of treatment could create low self-esteem, insecurity and they could become fearful, reducing their capacity for learning.

You can be sure that with these simple tips your pet and you will be extremely happy and close to each other. Besides, he or she will teach you many things to have a less complicated and stressful life with very simple behaviors that if you pay attention, you will understand immediately.

They always carry out their mission in this world and in our lives, remember those who are still missing for many different reasons. After all, they would give their life for you and they would ask in return just a little bit of love and a few minutes of your time. Remember too, that the great memories of all that lived with you in your life will accompany you forever.

about the author

Born as a Midtown girl in Manhattan, NY she grew in Mexico City metro area in a family who raised animals, that closeness to domestic animals allowed her to establish a special bond with them. Since very young she enjoyed going to countryside to visit her relative's farm where she could ride on donkeys, horses or run after chickens, goats and sheep.

During her life, she always has been accompanied by dogs, in them she could find the peace, comfort and love with nothing in return except for a pet and a good snack. In their eyes she could experienced the presence of God.

In her late teenage years was living between New York and Mexico City where she could work sitting kids and dogs, that's where she got in touch with different ways of relationship between humans and animals.

She studied the first year of Biology at the National Autonomous University of Mexico, to then later get the Bachelor's Degree in Optometry. Her interests in telling stories to her children stem the idea to start writing for kids.

She currently lives in an Atlanta GA, with her two children and husband and her beloved dog Almendrita.